Overcoming
Anxiety, Stress & Worry

A Caregiver's Guide

Dedication

To the caregivers who find themselves in uncharted territory, facing challenges for which they feel untrained and unprepared.

For those who navigate the anxiety, stress, and worry that come with caring for a loved one, this guide is for you. I celebrate your courage, strength, and compassion.

Be assured, you possess a strength far beyond your imagination.

Caregivers DO Matter.

"There are only four kinds of people in the world,

Those who have been *caregivers*.
Those who are current_y *caregivers*.
Those who will be *caregivers*,
and those who will need a *caregiver*.

— *Rosalynn Carter*

Contents

INTRODUCTION

Have you ever found yourself in a situation where you're juggling multiple responsibilities, none of which you were prepared for? When faced with these demands, you might feel a wave of nausea, shortness of breath, and a spinning head. It can be overwhelming, with too much to handle and not enough training to guide you through.

Caregiving often mirrors this experience. You frequently step into this role without any prior preparation or guidance. Your loved one requires attention, care, and comfort, but you may feel uncertain about how to meet those needs. This uncertainty can quickly lead to anxiety, stress and worry.

Every caregiver faces anxiety at some point. However, as caregiving progresses, this anxiety can escalate into a chronic condition, potentially leading to harmful physical effects. It's crucial to recognize the signs early and take action. Prioritizing self-care is vital for anyone in a caregiving role.

CHAPTER 1 — ANXIETY

A nxiety is a common emotion experienced by many people, including full-time caregivers. It is characterized by feelings of unease, apprehension, or worry, often accompanied by physical sensations such as sweating, trembling, or an increased heart rate.

For full-time caregivers, anxiety may be related to the stress and demands of providing care to a loved one who is ill, disabled, or elderly. Caregivers may experience anxiety about their ability to provide adequate care, concerns about the health and well-being of their loved one, financial pressures, or social isolation.

Anxiety Disorders: Common Types, Symptoms and Treatments

Yes, there are people whose brains are genetically wired to love thrills and risks. There was even a pop phrase for them that emerged a few decades back — Type T personalities. But for

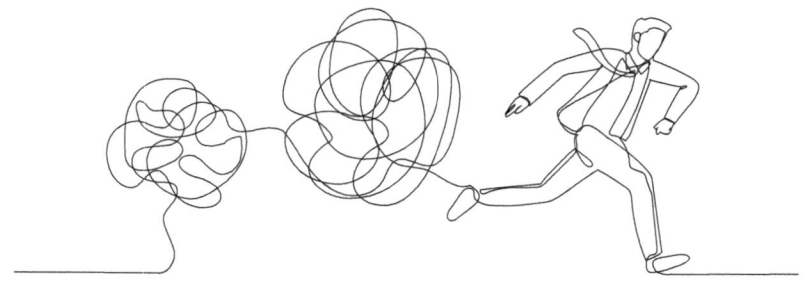

the majority of us, fear is hardly a favorite emotion. That doesn't mean we don't appreciate its role in protecting us from threats. The pounding heart and rapid breathing that accompany fear are important to the body's "fight or flight" response, which helps us take quick action in a crisis — and then, ideally, get back to a fear-free everyday life.

Anxiety — best defined as worrying about a potential threat — can be protective too. "Anxiety is a normal human emotion," says Robert Hudak, M.D., associate professor of psychiatry at the University of Pittsburgh. "Without anxiety, you wouldn't buckle your seatbelt on the way to work in the morning. You wouldn't look both ways before crossing the street."

Anxiety can become a problem when "the fear is out of proportion to the real threat," says Danielle Cooper, an assistant professor of clinical psychiatry at the Center for the Treatment and Study of Anxiety at the University of Pennsylvania. When a person chronically feels anxiety beyond what is reasonable and it interferes with normal life, doctors often diagnose this as an anxiety disorder. Symptoms include a pervasive sense of distress and physiological signs such as muscle tension, a rapid heartbeat, insomnia, stomach upset and shortness of breath. With an anxiety disorder, "the nervous system reacts as if there's a threat in the environment, when little or none exists," Hudak says.

The good news about anxiety disorders? They are treatable, at any stage of life.

Risk factors and triggers

Anxiety disorders can affect anyone, at any time in life, but there are predisposing factors, including a family history of anxiety, certain personality traits, stressful life events and social isolation. Women are more likely than men to suffer from an anxiety disorder, according to the National Institute of Mental Health.

Aging related health changes can provoke anxiety, too. People who have trouble hearing, for instance, might start worrying about not being able to join in conversations. In fact, older adults with hearing loss are more likely to have anxiety, research shows. Loss of physical functioning, or the ability to move about with ease, is another common trigger, says psychiatrist Ramaswamy Viswanathan, M.D., president elect of the American Psychiatric Association. Losing muscle strength can lead to a fear of falling, which can lead to moving less and being more afraid of falling — and so on, in a downward spiral. Concerns about limited finances and losing independence can weigh on older adults, too.

Having more time on your hands can cause long buried worries to bubble up. "When you're busy, [they] might not be at the forefront of your mind," Cooper says. But when you retire or are otherwise freed up from preoccupations, issues you avoided might get a foothold, triggering anxiety. [1]

[1] Learn about 4 common anxiety disorders – By Tania Hannan
Reviewed by Helen Lavretsky, M.D.
Published February 15, 2024
https://www.aarp.org/health/conditions-treatments/info-2024/anxiety-disorders.html

I Wish I Could Have Done Better

Claudia had always been a "Nervous Nellie." It was a title she wore like a badge of honor, even if it was a little tattered from years of wear. Her anxiety had woven itself into the fabric of her life, starting with that traumatic encounter with the family dog when she was just three years old. The memory was vivid: the dog's loud barking echoed in her ears, and the playful antics that had seemed so innocent to others had terrified her to the core.

Years later, Claudia found herself standing in the kitchen, a knot of anxiety tightening in her stomach as she prepared dinner for her mother, Diana. It was a routine she had grown accustomed to, yet each task felt like climbing a mountain. As she stirred the simmering pot, Yvonne, her coworker and neighbor, popped her head through the doorway.

"Hey, Claudia! Need any help?" Yvonne asked, her voice bright and cheerful.

Claudia forced a smile, though her heart raced. "No, I'm fine. Just trying to get dinner ready."

Yvonne stepped inside anyway, her warm smile unwavering. "You know, you can always ask for help. I don't bite!"

Claudia chuckled lightly, though the tension in her shoulders didn't ease. "It's just... I don't want to bother anyone."

"Bothering? That's what friends are for!" Yvonne said, leaning against the counter.

"You've been looking a bit stressed lately. Is everything okay with your mom?"

Claudia took a deep breath, her mind racing with thoughts of her mother's worsening condition. "Yeah, she's... she's alright. Just a little more forgetful these days."

"Claudia," Yvonne said gently, "you really should talk to someone about this. It can't be easy."

Claudia shook her head, her heart pounding. "I can't. I have everything under control."

But even as she said it, the truth felt like a lie.

Later that evening, Claudia's phone buzzed with a message from Todd, her on-and-off boyfriend. She stared at the screen, feeling a mix of anxiety and longing. She remembered their last conversation, filled with unspoken words and unresolved feelings.

"Hey, can we talk?" Todd had texted.

Claudia hesitated before replying. "Sure, what's up?"

When they met later at a café, the atmosphere was heavy with tension. Todd looked concerned as they sat down. "Claudia, I feel like you're always holding back. I can't help you if you don't let me in."

Claudia fidgeted with her coffee cup, the steam fogging her glasses. "It's just... I don't want to drag you into my mess."

"But I care about you," Todd insisted, leaning forward. "You don't have to handle everything alone."

"I know, but... sometimes it feels safer to keep things to myself," she admitted, her voice barely above a whisper.

Todd sighed, frustration flickering across his face. "You can't keep pushing me away. It's exhausting for both of us."

As they parted ways that evening, Claudia felt a familiar weight settle in her chest. She wanted to open up, but the thought of vulnerability terrified her. Days turned into weeks, and their relationship grew distant, each conversation laced with unspoken fears until they finally drifted apart.

Back at home, Claudia found herself in the role of caregiver for her mother, who struggled with chronic health issues. Diana had always been the steady one, but now Claudia felt the weight of the world on her shoulders. Dinner preparations turned into panic sessions as she worried about her mother's medication schedule.

"Mom, did you take your pills today?" Claudia asked one evening, her voice tinged with anxiety.

Diana looked up from her chair, confusion clouding her eyes. "I think so, dear. Did I?"

Claudia's heart raced. "I'll just check the pill organizer. Can you try to remember for me?"

Diana nodded, but Claudia could see the frustration in her mother's eyes. "I'm trying, Claudia. I really am."

"I WISH I COULD HAVE DONE BETTER."

"I know, Mom. It's just... I don't want anything to happen to you," Claudia said, her voice breaking.

As the weeks turned into months, the anxiety continued to spiral. Every bump in the night sent Claudia into panic attacks, her heart racing as she imagined the worst. It was a cycle that left her exhausted and worn. Meanwhile, Yvonne's concern grew.

"Claudia, please," Yvonne urged one afternoon at work, "you need to talk to someone.

This isn't just about your mom anymore."

"I can't! I'm fine. I can handle it," Claudia retorted, her voice rising in frustration.

"Handling things doesn't mean pushing everyone away," Yvonne replied softly. "You're not alone in this."

But Claudia felt alone. As her mother's condition worsened, the anxiety became unbearable. She found herself spiraling deeper into a pit she couldn't climb out of. One night, after a particularly difficult day, Claudia sat on the edge of her bed, tears streaming down her face. She felt as if the walls were closing in.

The next day, things took a turn for the worse. Diana fell and broke her hip, and Claudia was forced to confront the reality of her mother's declining health. After a frantic trip to the hospital, the doctor sat down with Claudia, his expression grave.

"Claudia, your mother needs more care than you can provide at home. I recommend considering a nursing home," he said gently.

Claudia's heart sank. "No... I can't do that. I can take care of her."

"Claudia, you have to think about what's best for both of you," he insisted. "She needs professional help."

As she sat in the hospital room, watching her mother sleep, Claudia felt a crushing weight of guilt and despair. "I'm so sorry, Mom," she whispered, her voice breaking.

Days later, they made the difficult decision to place Diana in a nursing home. Claudia visited often, but the guilt gnawed at her. She felt she had failed in her role as caregiver, unable to protect her mother from the ravages of age and illness.

"Claudia, it's okay to feel this way," Yvonne said during one of her visits. "You did your best."

"I should have been stronger," Claudia replied, tears spilling down her cheeks. "I should have been able to handle it."

"Sometimes, strength means knowing when to ask for help," Yvonne said, her voice soothing yet firm.

But Claudia couldn't hear it. In her mind, she had already lost everything—her mother, her relationship with Todd, and any semblance of control over her life.

Months passed, and as the cold winter air settled in, Claudia received the call she had dreaded. Her mother had passed away peacefully in her sleep. The news shattered what little remained of Claudia's fragile spirit.

Standing by her mother's grave, she felt a profound emptiness envelop her. "I'm so sorry, Mom," she whispered into the biting wind. "I wish I could have done better."

As she turned to leave, the weight of her unspoken fears and unresolved anxieties felt heavier than ever. Claudia had always been a "Nervous Nellie," but now she stood alone, grappling with the reality that she had refused to confront for so long. The path ahead felt dark, and the thought of seeking help remained an insurmountable hurdle.

Alone with her thoughts, she walked away, the echoes of her mother's love lingering in the air, a reminder of what she had lost and what she had never been able to share.

Common anxiety disorders
There are four common types of anxiety disorders:

1.) Generalized anxiety disorder

People who have *generalized anxiety disorder*, or GAD, worry intensely about lots of things and tend to expect the worst. They have a hard time containing their fear, even when they realize it's not rational. People with GAD may try to control situations and believe, consciously or unconsciously, that worrying somehow protects them.

> ## "PANIC ATTACKS ARE SUDDEN EPISODES OF INTENSE FEAR."

GAD is the most common type of anxiety disorder in older adults. Besides worry, symptoms include irritability, trouble sleeping, a rapid heart rate, rapid breathing, weakness or fatigue and difficulty concentrating. Ongoing headaches or stomachaches are also common.

2.) Social anxiety disorder

Everyone has felt self-conscious or embarrassed in front of others — but people with social anxiety disorder have an intense fear of being watched, judged or rejected. Some people fear social situations across the board, while others fear situations in which they have to speak or otherwise perform in front of others.

People with social anxiety disorder often avoid interacting with others. When they can't steer clear, they experience extreme distress, including a rapid heart rate, blushing, trembling, feeling their mind go blank and nausea. Without treatment, social anxiety disorder can have profound effects on a person's social life and work life.

3.) Panic disorder

Panic attacks are sudden episodes of intense fear that involve extreme symptoms, such as sweating, chest pain, shortness of breath, choking sensations, dizziness and nausea, along with feelings of impending doom or death. They're as scary as they sound. It's common for people experiencing panic attacks to end up in an emergency room. Yet, unlike heart attacks, panic attacks typically subside within about 20 minutes.

Panic disorder is diagnosed when people who experience panic attacks become consumed with the fear of having another one. Panic disorder and agoraphobia, the fear of being in a place or situation in which you can't escape or get help, often occur together.

4.) Specific phobias

Heights, flying, snakes, needles, dental work — these things make many of us nervous, even scared. But people who have a phobia go to great lengths to avoid the object of their fear. People with a phobia feel powerless to control it, even when they recognize the fear is not based in reality. Symptoms such as rapid heartbeat, nausea, dizziness, fainting and difficulty breathing typically accompany phobias.

Phobias often start early in life, but they can occur any time. Among elderly adults, falling is a common phobia. Although phobias sometimes develop after a traumatic experience, they can also appear out of the blue. [2]

---

[2] Learn about 4 common anxiety disorders – By Tania Hannan
Reviewed by Helen Lavretsky, M.D.
Published February 15, 2024
https://www.aarp.org/health/conditions-treatments/info-2024/anxiety-disorders.html

Accidental Anxiety

Rashidi had always taken pride in his calm demeanor and unshakeable composure. For years, he dedicated himself to mastering the intricate movements of martial arts, immersing himself in the discipline and philosophy that accompanied each technique. His precision extended beyond physical combat; he became an expert sharpshooter at the gun range, where every shot was a witness to his focus and unwavering concentration.

Academically, he had also excelled, earning a master's degree in psychology from Villanova University, where he delved deep into the complexities of the human mind. This combination of physical prowess and intellectual insight made him a formidable individual, someone who had navigated countless challenges with grace and resilience.

Yet, despite his extensive training and experiences, nothing could have truly prepared Rashidi for the ordeal that lay ahead. As he stood on the face of an unforeseen crisis, he sensed that the trials he would soon face would test the very core of his character. He would need every ounce of strength and wisdom he had cultivated to confront the storm that was approaching.

Rashidi and his wife, Sameera, who have been together for nineteen years, cherished their "stress free" lifestyle. They frequently spent their leisure time in nature, cycling along the Kelly Drive by the Schuylkill River, where they loved to watch the geese soar in formation from one bank to the other.

Their four children were considerate enough to look after one another, allowing their parents a much needed break from daily routines. Aged between twelve and eighteen, they managed to keep the household in order, handling everything from cooking and cleaning to gardening and maintaining a beautifully kept yard.

Life had once felt perfect for Rashidi and Sameera's family. The occasional squabbles among the siblings and the rare miscommunications between Rashidi and Sameera were simply the ebb and flow of family life. Overall, their household thrived on love, laughter, and an unshakeable bond that seemed to weather any storm.

But fate can be cruel and unpredictable. One fateful evening, as Sameera was driving home after a long, exhausting day at work, she envisioned a peaceful night ahead with her devoted husband and their children.

However, in a tragic twist, a drunk driver veered into her lane on the notorious Lincoln Drive, resulting in a catastrophic head on collision. The aftermath of this horrific accident was devastating. Sameera was left paralyzed from the waist down, thrust into a world of uncertainty and trauma that shattered the life they had built together.

Rashidi was reeling from the shock, grappling with a whirlwind of emotions. He felt the weight of a heavy burden upon his shoulders, knowing he had to be the pillar of strength for Sameera and their children during this unimaginable crisis.

In the days following the accident, Rashidi felt as if he were moving through a fog. The vibrant, energetic woman he had loved for years was now reliant on a wheelchair, and he struggled to reconcile this new reality. The responsibility of caring for Sameera, coupled with the needs of their children, felt overwhelming.

Each family member was processing the trauma in their own way, and Rashidi was acutely aware of the emotional turmoil that lay beneath the surface.

As the weeks turned into months, Rashidi's anxiety escalated. He was constantly preoccupied with thoughts about Sameera's physical rehabilitation and emotional healing, as well as the ripple effect of her accident on their children's lives. It felt as if he were walking on a tightrope, perpetually anxious that even a minor misstep could lead to further disaster.

At the same time, Rashidi faced mounting pressures at work as a dedicated teacher at Central

High School. His passion for education had always driven him, but now, he found it increasingly difficult to manage his teaching responsibilities alongside the demands of home life. The delicate balance he once maintained felt like it was slipping away, leaving him exhausted and frazzled.

The stress began to manifest physically and mentally. Nights turned restless, filled with worry and sleeplessness, while days were punctuated by sudden panic attacks that left him breathless. Rashidi wore a brave face for his family and colleagues, but inside, he felt as if he were unraveling.

Eventually, the weight of his struggles became too much to bear alone. Recognizing the need for support, Rashidi sought help from a therapist who specialized in assisting caregivers. This decision marked a turning point in his journey. He also began medication to help stabilize his symptoms, a step that opened the door to healing.

Gradually, Rashidi learned strategies to better manage his anxiety. He carved out moments for self-care, whether it was an early morning run or a brief meditation during lunch. He discovered the importance of reaching out for assistance, whether from friends, family, or colleagues. This new found willingness to accept help was liberating, allowing him to share the load instead of carrying it all alone.

As time passed, Rashidi and his family began to establish a new normal. They navigated the complexities of life with a family member living with a disability, transforming their challenges into opportunities for growth. The bonds among them deepened as they learned to lean on one another for support.

Though Rashidi still faced moments of anxiety, he now possessed the tools and the support system necessary to confront them. He understood that this journey, burdened with obstacles, was also a path toward resilience and connection, ultimately enriching their lives in ways he could never have anticipated. Together, they moved forward, stronger and more united than ever.

"EVERY CAREGIVER FACES ANXIETY AT SOME POINT."

Anxiety is a common experience for caregivers, as caregiving can be a challenging and sometimes overwhelming responsibility.

Here are some ways that anxiety can present itself in caregiving:

Physical symptoms: Anxiety can manifest in physical symptoms such as fatigue, headaches, muscle tension, and trouble sleeping.

Constant worry: Caregivers may worry about the health and safety of their loved one, financial concerns, and the future.

Feeling overwhelmed: Caregivers may feel like there is too much to do and not enough time to do it, leading to feelings of overwhelm and stress.

Guilt: Caregivers may feel guilty if they take time for themselves or if they feel like they are not doing enough.

Social isolation: Caregivers may feel socially isolated if they are unable to participate in social activities or if they feel like they cannot leave their loved one alone.

Some strategies for managing anxiety in caregiving include:

Seeking support: Talking to friends, family members, or a therapist can help caregivers manage their anxiety and stress.

Taking breaks: Caregivers should take time for themselves to engage in activities they enjoy, such as reading, exercising, or spending time with friends.

Prioritizing tasks: Caregivers should prioritize tasks and consider delegating tasks to others when possible.

Learning relaxation techniques: Deep breathing, meditation, and progressive muscle relaxation can help caregivers manage stress and anxiety.

Practicing self-care: Caregivers should make sure they are taking care of their physical and emotional needs, including eating well, getting enough sleep, and engaging in self-care activities.

Being a caregiver can be demanding and anxiety can have a significant impact on a caregiver's physical and emotional well-being.

Here are some ways anxiety can affect a caregiver:

Physical symptoms: Anxiety can cause physical symptoms such as headaches, muscle tension, fatigue, upset stomach, and difficulty sleeping. These symptoms can make it more challenging to provide care effectively and can reduce the overall quality of life for the caregiver.

Emotional distress: Caregivers can experience a range of emotions, including sadness, anger, frustration, guilt, and helplessness. Anxiety can intensify these emotions and make it difficult for caregivers to manage their feelings in a healthy way.

Decreased ability to provide care: Caregivers who are experiencing anxiety may find it more challenging to provide care effectively. They may have difficulty focusing, making decisions, and carrying out tasks efficiently, which can negatively impact the person they are caring for.

Increased risk of burnout: Caregiver burnout is a state of physical, emotional, and mental exhaustion that can occur when caregivers experience chronic stress and feel overwhelmed by their caregiving responsibilities. Anxiety can increase the risk of burnout, as caregivers may struggle to manage their stress levels effectively.

Overall, anxiety can have a significant impact on a caregiver's ability to provide care effectively. It's essential for caregivers to prioritize their own self-care and seek support when needed to manage their anxiety and maintain their well-being.

Frequently Asked Questions: (FAQs)

What are some common causes of anxiety in caregivers?

Increased responsibility and commitment, financial strain, lack of support and social isolation, and high expectations.

How does anxiety affect full-time caregivers?

Anxiety can cause physical and emotional symptoms, increase the risk of health problems, and negatively affect efficacy in caregiving roles.

How can full-time caregivers manage their anxiety?

They can practice self-care and stress management, seek support and help, and set realistic expectations for themselves.

Can caregivers experience positive results over time with the management of anxiety?

Yes, caregivers can experience better physical and emotional health, reduced stress levels, and improved caregiving roles with consistent self-care and supportive strategies.

Where can caregivers find resources and support for managing anxiety?

Caregivers can find resources and support through family, friends, healthcare providers, counseling/therapy services, and networks with fellow caregivers.

CHAPTER 2 — STRESS

S tress is the body's natural response to a perceived threat or demand. It can manifest in various ways, including physical, emotional, and behavioral symptoms, and can be caused by both positive and negative events. Stress is a part of life and can be beneficial in small doses, but chronic stress can have detrimental effects on physical and mental health.

For full-time caregivers, stress is a common experience. The demands and responsibilities that come with caring for a loved one can leave caregivers feeling overwhelmed, anxious, and emotionally drained.

As a caregiver, taking care of a loved one can bring joy and fulfillment into your life, but it can also bring a lot of stress. Caregiver stress is prevalent, but it is often over looked and poorly understood. Long term stress can lead to serious health problems for the caregiver such as depression, anxiety, high blood pressure, and heart disease. Caregivers must balance the needs of their loved ones with their own needs and responsibilities. This balancing act can be difficult and can cause significant stress. In this section we will explore the causes, effects, signs, and solutions to caregiver stress.

Causes of Caregiver Stress

Caregivers can experience stress for a number of reasons, including lack of support, isolation, financial strain, and dealing with complex medical issues. Providing care for a loved one can be isolating, and caregivers often feel alone and unsupported. Financial stress is another common cause of caregiver stress. When a caregiver is unable to work full-time and must rely on savings or support from other family members, it can cause significant stress. Another cause of caregiver stress is dealing with complex medical issues. Caregivers must manage medications, appointments, and complicated medical procedures, which can be overwhelming and stressful.

Effects of Caregiver Stress

Long-term stress can lead to serious health problems for the caregiver such as depression, anxiety, high blood pressure, and heart disease. However, the effects of caregiver stress are not limited to physical health. It can also lead to emotional exhaustion and burnout. Caregivers often feel guilty when they take time for themselves, which can lead to resentfulness and anger. Caregivers may also become withdrawn and disconnected from friends and family members, leading to social isolation and loneliness.

Signs of Caregiver Stress

It can be difficult for caregivers to recognize when they are experiencing stress. Signs of stress can include difficulty sleeping, lack of energy, feelings of hopelessness, and irritability. Caregivers may also experience physical symptoms such as headaches, back pain, and gastrointestinal problems. Additionally, caregivers who are experiencing stress may withdraw from social activities or have difficulty concentrating.

Wishing Things Were Different

It has been a year since Teisha took on the role of being her mother's full-time caregiver. Teisha had no idea how much it would affect her mental, emotional, and physical well-being. What started as a simple act of love and care became a severe source of stress that haunts her every day.

Teisha's mother Louise had always been her closest confidante and ally. She was the strong one who supported Teisha through her mind boggling projects in college. As the years passed, Louise developed some health issues that she didn't quite attend to well enough. One day, she had a massive heart attack that left her dependent on others for her daily tasks. Teisha wanted to repay the debt of kindness and care that her mother had given her all these years, so she became her mother's full-time caregiver.

Teisha felt the weight of the world on her shoulders as she stepped into her mother's room, noticing the tired lines etched on her face. Louise, her mother, sat in a chair, clutching a photograph album with her frail hands. Teisha took a deep breath and mustered a smile.

"Good morning, Mom. How are you feeling today?" she asked, hoping to keep the conversation light.

Louise looked up; her eyes distant yet searching. "I don't know, Teisha. I'm scared. I feel like I'm losing myself."

Teisha's heart sank. She sat down next to her mother and held her hand. "You're not alone, Mom. I'm here for you, always."

Louise nodded, tears welling in her eyes. "I know, Teisha. But I see how tired you are. You're trying to do it all, and it's breaking my heart."

A sigh escaped Teisha's lips, her voice tinged with exhaustion. "I thought I had a support system, Mom, but they've backed out one by one. Where are these so called friends when you need them most?"

Louise's voice trembled with sadness. "I never wanted this burden for you, my dear. I never wanted to be a source of stress and hardship."

Tears streamed down Teisha's face, her voice choked with emotion. "You're not, Mom. It's not your fault.

I just wish things were different."

They sat in silence for a moment, their shared pain hanging heavy in the room. Then, Louise spoke softly, her words filled with resignation. "Sometimes life doesn't give us the happy ending we hope for, Teisha. We have to find strength in the midst of the storms."

Teisha wiped away her tears, her voice quivering. "I'm trying, Mom. But it's so hard. I feel like I'm drowning."

Louise reached out and held her daughter's face, her touch gentle and filled with love. "You're stronger than you know, my dear. Remember to take care of yourself, too. Your well-being matters."

Teisha nodded, her voice filled with determination.

"I won't give up, Mom. I'll keep fighting for us."

As the days turned into weeks and the weeks into months, Teisha's burden grew heavier. The stress continued to mount, taking a toll on her physical and mental health. She tried her best to find moments of respite, but the weight of her responsibilities threatened to crush her.

From running errands to performing personal hygiene tasks, Teisha became the sole caregiver. She even had to quit her full-time job and switch to a part-time one. Despite all her efforts, the caregiving tasks never seem to end, as her mother's condition worsens over with time.

What's more, the support she was counting on didn't show up when she needed them the most. Friends and family members who promised to assist her, backed out, leaving Teisha bitter and exhausted.

Teisha feels like she's reached the end of her rope.

Teisha's mom Louise knows how much care Teisha has given her and how much stress that has caused her. Teisha confided in her about feeling overwhelmed and alone. Louise urged her daughter to "never give up," and encouraged her to continue being strong and have faith. However, even as Teisha tried to maintain a positive outlook, it just became too much for her to bear.

Bills pile up as she struggles to make ends meet while caring for her mother. It just seems like there's no happy ending to this story.

Louise, seeing her daughter's anguish, held her hand and whispered, "I'm sorry, Teisha. I'm sorry for the pain I'm causing you.'"

Teisha's voice was filled with love and desperation. "Don't apologize, Mom. You have nothing to be sorry for. I just wish I could do more for you."

Louise's voice grew weaker, her eyes reflecting deep weariness. "You've done more than enough, my dear. I'm proud of you."

In the end, despite Teisha's unwavering dedication, the story didn't have a happy ending. The weight of caregiving became too much for her to bear, and the financial strain took its toll. Teisha had to make the heartbreaking decision to transition her mother to a nursing home, where professional caregivers could provide the round-the-clock care, she needed.

As Teisha visited Louise in the nursing home, tears filled her eyes. "I'm sorry, Mom. I tried my best."

Louise smiled weakly, her voice barely a whisper. "You did, my dear. You did more than anyone could ask for. Remember, life doesn't always give us happy endings. But you showed me love until the very end, and that's what matters."

And with those words, Louise closed her eyes, her journey in this world coming to an end. Teisha's heart shattered, forever marked by the tremendous stress and the bittersweet love she had experienced as a caregiver. She carried the weight of her mother's memory with her, a testament to the sacrifices and challenges faced by caregivers who give their all, even in the absence of a happy ending. Teisha's story is the reality of life as a full-time caregiver. It's also one that's not often talked about, making it difficult for caregivers like Teisha to seek help and support. That's why it's important for all of us to acknowledge the selfless sacrifice that caregivers make in looking after their loved ones. We should extend a helping hand and provide social support whenever we can.

Difference between stress and distress

Stress is a normal reaction to challenges in your physical environment or in your perceptions of what's happening around you. Experts consider distress to be stress that is severe, prolonged, or both. Distress is when you feel you're under more stress than you can handle.

"IT IS IMPORTANT FOR CAREGIVERS
TO DELEGATE TASKS."

Emotional Stress Symptoms

Mental symptoms of emotional stress include:

- Feeling more emotional than usual, especially feeling grumpy, teary, or angry
- Feeling anxious, overwhelmed, nervous, or on edge
- Feeling sad or depressed
- Feeling restless
- Trouble keeping track of or remembering things
- Trouble getting your work done, solving problems, making decisions, or concentrating

Physical Stress Symptoms

Symptoms of stress that you might feel in your body include:

- Headaches, Dizziness
- Clenching your jaw and grinding your teeth
- Shoulder, neck, or back pain; general body aches, pains, and tense muscles
- Chest pain, increased heart rate, heaviness in your chest
- Shortness of breath
- Feeling more tired than usual (fatigue)
- Sleeping more or less than usual
- Upset stomach, including diarrhea, constipation, and nausea
- Loss of sexual desire and/or ability
- Getting sick more easily; getting colds and infections often

Respiratory distress

This is when you aren't getting enough oxygen or arehaving to work really hard to breathe. If you or a loved one has symptoms of respiratory distress, you need to call 911 and get to the ER as soon as possible. *Signs include:*

- Breathing faster than usual
- Color changes of your skin, mouth, lips, or fingernails.

A blue color around your mouth, lips, or fingernails usually shows you aren't getting enough oxygen. Your skin may also look pale or gray.

- Grunting when you breath out
- A whistling with each breath (wheezing)
- Nose flaring
- Chest sinking below your neck or under your breastbone with each breath (retractions)
- Increased sweating, especially cold, clammy skin on your forehead
- Leaning forward while sitting to help take deeper breaths

Cognitive Stress Symptoms
Symptoms of stress that affect your mental performance include:

- Trouble keeping track of or remembering things
- Trouble getting your work done, solving problems, making decisions, or concentrating
- Feeling less commitment to your work
- Lack of motivation
- Negative thinking

Behavioral Stress Symptoms
Symptoms of behavioral stress include:

- Changes in your eating habits; losing or gaining weight
- Procrastinating and avoiding responsibilities
- Using alcohol, tobacco, or drugs to feel better
- Avoiding your friends and family; isolating yourself from others
- Failing to meet your deadlines
- Increased absences at school or work
- Doing your work more slowly
- Exercising less often

Overcoming Caregiver Stress

There are several things caregivers can do to manage their stress. Seeking support from friends, family members, or support groups can be helpful. Caregivers should also prioritize taking time for themselves, whether that means going for a walk or spending time with friends. Engaging in regular exercise, maintaining a healthy diet, and getting enough sleep can also aid in managing stress. Furthermore, it is important for caregivers to delegate tasks and ask for help when needed.

Symptoms of Chronic Stress

Chronic stress is when you experience stress over an extended time. This can have negative effects on your body and your mental state, and it can increase your risk of cardiovascular disease, anxiety, and depression.

In general, the symptoms of chronic stress are the same as those for shorter term stress. You may not have all these symptoms, but if you have more than three symptoms and they last for a few weeks, you may have chronic stress. Potential symptoms to look for include:

- Aches and pains
- Changes in your sleeping patterns, such as insomnia or sleepiness
- Changes in your social behavior, such as avoiding other people
- Changes in your emotional response to others
- Emotional withdrawal
- Low energy, fatigue
- Unfocused or cloudy thinking
- Changes in your appetite
- Increased alcohol or drug use
- Getting sick more often than usual

Is It Stress or Something Else?

You may be dealing with something more serious than day-to-day stress if you have symptoms over a period of time even though you've tried to cope using healthy mechanisms. Long-term stress is linked to number of mental health disorders, such as:

- Chronic stress
- Anxiety
- Depression
- Substance use disorder
- Disordered eating

It may be time to visit your doctor if you're struggling to cope with the stress in your life or you have mental health problems from long-term stress. They can help you figure out ways of coping in a healthy way or refer you to a mental health professional who can help you.

Posttraumatic Stress Disorder

Posttraumatic stress disorder (PTSD) is mental health condition that you may have after you have or witness a traumatic event, such as a natural disaster, accident, or violence. PTSD overwhelms your ability to cope with new stress. PTSD can lead to symptoms such as intrusive memories, avoidance behaviors, and hyperarousal.

These symptoms can cause significant problems in your work or relationships. Talk to your doctor or a mental health professional if you've had or witnessed a traumatic event and have disturbing thoughts and feelings about it for more than a month, if your thoughts and feelings are severe, or if you feel like you're having trouble getting your life back on track.

What Are the Consequences of Long-Term Stress?

Ongoing, chronic stress can trigger or worsen many serious health problems, including:

- Mental health problems, such as depression, anxiety, and personality disorders
- Cardiovascular disease, including heart disease, high blood pressure, abnormal heart rhythms, heart attacks, and strokes
- Obesity and other eating disorders
- Menstrual problems
- Sexual dysfunction, such as impotence and premature ejaculation in men and loss of sexual desire in men and women
- Skin and hair problems, such as acne, psoriasis, and eczema, and permanent hair loss

---

"STRESS IS A PART OF LIFE."

Gastrointestinal problems, such as GERD, gastritis, ulcerative colitis, and irritable bowel syndrome

Help Is Available for Stress

Stress is a part of life. What matters most is how you handle it. The best thing you can do to prevent stress overload and the health consequences that come with it is to know your stress symptoms.

If you or a loved one is feeling overwhelmed by stress, talk to your doctor. Many symptoms of stress can also be signs of other health problems. Your doctor can evaluate your symptoms and rule out other conditions. If stress is to blame, your doctor can recommend a therapist or counselor to help you better handle your stress.

Stress Takeaways

Stress is your body's response to a challenging or demand-ing situation. It can affect you physically, mentally, and behaviorally,especiallywhenyouhavechronicstress.Chronicstress is when you are stressed for an extended time. Chronic stress can make it more likely for you to develop other mental health disorders, such as anxiety or depression. It can also affect your heart health and digestive health. If you're stressed and having trouble coping, it may be time for you to see your doctor or a mental health professional. [1]

[1] Stress Symptoms By Hedy Marks;Lori M. King, PhD
Medically Reviewed by Shruthi N, MD on June 19, 2024
 https://www.webmd.com/balance/stress-management/stress-symptoms-effects_of-stress-on-the-body

Silently Stressing

James walked down the hall, the smell of coffee mingling with the faint aroma of toast. He glanced at the clock—it was almost time for his father, J.C., to wake up. The rhythmic beeping of the blood sugar monitor in the corner provided a backdrop to his morning routine, a reminder of the delicate balance he had to maintain. "Dad, time to rise and shine!" James called out, pouring a steaming cup of coffee into a thermos. J.C. grumbled in response, the sound muffled by the layers of blankets he had cocooned himself in. "Five more minutes, Jim," he replied, his voice thick with sleep. James chuckled softly. "I'll give you five minutes, but then we need to get moving.

Your doctor's appointment is at nine, and I don't want to keep Dr. Miller waiting."

With a sigh, J.C. finally swung his legs over the side of the bed. "You're too much like your mother. Always on time. I swear, if she were here, she'd have me up at dawn." James felt a pang at the mention of his mother. She had always been the one who organized everything, keeping the family on track. "Well, I learned from the best," he said lightly, forcing a smile. "Now, let's get you dressed."

As they moved through the morning routine, J.C. struggled to fasten his shirt. James knelt down beside him, gently guiding his hands. "Here, let me help you with that," he said, his voice steady. "Thanks, son. I don't know what I'd do without you," J.C. admitted, a hint of vulnerability creeping into his tone. "Say less," James blurted out with a smile. "You don't have to worry about that, Dad. I've got this," James replied, though internally, he felt the weight of his responsibilities pressing down on him.

Each day was a balancing act—medications, meals, physical therapy, and appointments. James had become a master at keeping everything spinning, like a circus performer with plates on sticks, but the stress began to mount.

At work, he was known as Jim, the reliable manager who could handle any crisis. He had always thrived in that role, but now, he felt like he was barely keeping it together. "Jim, you, okay?" asked his colleague, Sarah, one afternoon as they reviewed a project together. "You seem a bit off lately." James forced a smile. "Just a lot on my plate. You know how it is." "Yeah, but if you need to talk or take a break, just let me know," Sarah offered, her concern genuine. "Thanks, but I'm fine. Really," he insisted, though inside he felt the familiar weight of cognitive stress creeping in, making it harder to concentrate.

One evening, after a particularly long day, James sank into the couch, exhaustion washing over him. J.C. was already asleep in the recliner across the room. The silence was comforting, but it also felt suffocating. He picked up his phone, scrolling through messages, and stumbled upon an article about stress management through counseling. "Maybe I should look into that," he muttered to himself.

The next day, James hesitantly approached his manager, Tom, during a break. "Hey, Tom, do you think the company offers any resources for counseling? I've been feeling a bit overwhelmed lately." Tom raised an eyebrow, concern etched on his face. "I didn't know you were struggling, Jim. We do have an Employee Assistance Program. I can get you the information if you want." "Yeah, I think that would help," James replied, feeling a flicker of hope.

A few weeks later, after several sessions with a counselor, James began to see changes. "It's like I've been holding my breath for so long," he confessed during one session. "I didn't realize how much I needed to talk about everything." His counselor nodded, encouraging him to explore his feelings. "It's important to express your concerns and not bottle them up. You're doing the right thing by seeking help."

Results of Overcoming Caregiver Stress

When caregivers are able to manage their stress effectively, it can have significant positive effects on their health and well-being. Caregivers may feel less overwhelmed and more in control of their lives. They may also have more energy and be better able to provide care for their loved ones.

Managing stress can also improve relationships with family and friends, and caregivers may find that they are better able to enjoy life outside of their caregiving responsibilities.

"CAREGIVERS MUST TAKE STEPS TO MANAGE THEIR STRESS."

How to Handle Caregiver Stress

Handling caregiver stress requires a combination of strategies. Caregivers must prioritize self-care, which includes exercise, healthy eating, and getting enough sleep. It is also important to seek support from friends, family members, or support groups. Caregivers should also consider asking for help when they need it. Taking time for oneself is also important, whether that means going for a walk or spending time with friends.

Caregiver stress is a prevalent issue that can have serious consequences for the caregiver. Therefore, caregivers must take steps to manage their stress. This includes seeking support from family and friends, prioritizing self-care, and delegating tasks. By effectively managing their stress, caregivers can improve their health and well being and provide better care for their loved ones.

Frequently Asked Questions:

What causes caregiver stress?

Caregiver stress can be caused by lack of support, isolation, financial strain, and dealing with complex medical issues.

What are the signs of caregiver stress?

Signs of caregiver stress can include difficulty sleeping, lack of energy, feelings of hopelessness, and irritability.

What can caregivers do to manage their stress?

Caregivers can manage their stress by seeking support from friends and family members, prioritizing self-care, and delegating tasks.

What are the effects of caregiver stress?

Long-term stress can lead to serious health problems for the caregiver such as depression, anxiety, high blood pressure, and heart disease.

How can managing stress improve caregivers' lives?

Managing stress can improve caregivers' lives by helping them feel less overwhelmed and more in control of their lives. They may also have more energy and be better able to provide care for their loved ones.

"EXTREME STRESS, CAN CAUSE EMOTIONAL DISTRESS."

Stress FAQs

What can extreme stress cause?

Extreme stress, especially if it's prolonged, can cause emotional distress. And stress from a traumatic event, which is usually extreme, can cause posttraumatic stress disorder (PTSD). These are more serious cases of stress that overwhelm your ability to manage on your own. You may need to get a professional's help to get back on track. If you feel like you're having trouble managing your emotions, talk to your doctor. They can help you or direct you to someone who can help you.

Can stress make you throw up?

Yes, stress can make you throw up. Your digestive system is one of the many systems that stress can affect. In fact, you may have a whole range of other digestive symptoms, such as nausea, pain, and constipation or diarrhea. Not everyone has stress nausea or vomiting, but you may be more prone to it if you have a gastrointestinal condition, such as irritable bowel syndrome (IBS), or you have anxiety or depression.

You may be able to tell if you're stress vomiting if your episode passes when the stress goes away. If it doesn't, then your episode may be caused by something else. It's time to get checked out by your doctor if you have more than a couple of episodes or you can't figure out what's causing them. [2]

[2] Stress Symptoms By Hedy Marks;Lori M. King, PhD
Medically Reviewed by Shruthi N, MD on June 19, 2024
https://www.webmd.com/balance/stress-management/stress-symptoms-effects_of_stress-on-the-body

CHAPTER 3 — WORRY

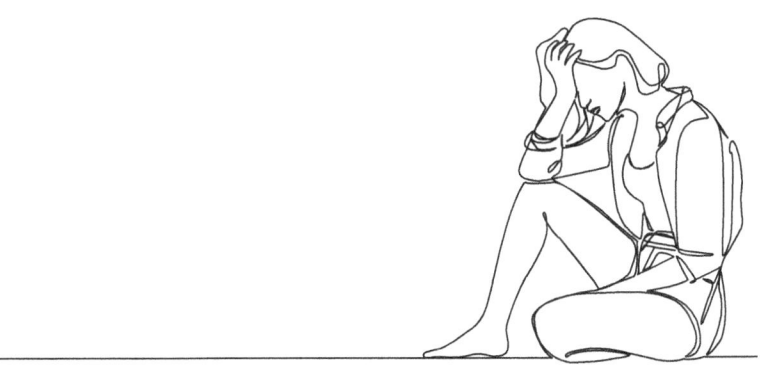

For a full-time caregiver, worry can be a constant state of concern, apprehension, or unease related to their caregiving responsibilities. It involves being preoccupied with the well-being, health, safety, and overall quality of life of the person they are caring for. Worry may arise from various factors, such as the physical or emotional health of the care recipient, managing daily tasks and routines, financial or logistical challenges, and the caregiver's own physical and emotional well-being. It can be an ongoing and exhausting aspect of being a full-time caregiver, often requiring support and self-care strategies to manage.

As a full-time caregiver, daily responsibilities can range from cooking and cleaning to administering medication and providing emotional support. While the role of a caregiver can be fulfilling, it can also be emotionally taxing and physically demanding. Full-time caregivers often experience worry, which can have negative effects on their physical and emotional wellbeing. In this article, we will explore the causes of worry on them, the effects of worry on caregivers, signs of worry, ways to overcome it, and how to handle worry as a full-time caregiver.

Causes of Worry in Full-Time Caregivers

Financial Burden: Providing full-time care often means leaving one's job and losing a source of income. This can lead to financial strain and worry about how to make ends meet.

Additionally, the cost of healthcare and medication can be overwhelming, especially for those without insurance.

Social Isolation: Full-time caregivers often have limited social interaction outside of their care responsibilities. They may feel isolated from friends and family, resulting in worry about the lack of support and feeling alone in their caregiver role.

Unpredictable Future: Caregivers often face an uncertain future, and this can cause worry. The care receiver's condition may worsen, ultimately leading to the end of their life. This unpredictability can be a source of constant worry and anxiety for the caregiver.

Care Receiver's Condition: The health of the care receiver can be a significant source of worry for full-time caregivers. Caregivers may worry about their loved one's condition worsening, not being able to provide the necessary care, or not being able to meet their loved one's changing needs.

Effects of Worry on Full-Time Caregivers

Physical Effects: Worry can take a toll on a caregiver's physical health. Chronic worry can lead to sleep disturbances, headaches, fatigue, and even digestive problems. Caregivers may also neglect their own health and well-being, leading to greater health problems down the line.

Emotional Effects: Worry can also affect a caregiver's emotional well-being. It can lead to feelings of anxiety, depression, and anger. Caregivers may feel overwhelmed, burned out and hopeless. Ultimately, these feelings can impact a caregiver's ability to provide quality care to their loved one.

Social Effects: Worry can also lead to social isolation, impacting a caregiver's relationship with family and friends. It may become increasingly difficult to maintain social connections, and as a result, caregivers may withdraw and feel even more isolated.

Signs of Worry in Full-Time Caregivers

Changes in Behavior: Caregivers experiencing worry may display changes in behavior, such as becoming irritable, agitated, or short tempered. They may also have difficulty concentrating or making decisions.

Physical Symptoms: Chronic worry can also result in physical symptoms, such as headaches, muscle tension, and digestive issues.

Negative Thoughts and Emotions: Caregivers may experience negative thoughts and emotions associated with their role, such as guilt, resentment, and fear.

Why We Worry and 6 Ways to Deal With It

It helps to acknowledge your worry and focus on what you can control.

It can feel overwhelming right now. One mental state that I'd bet we have all experienced recently is worry. With so much change happening in every facet of life, it's normal to feel worried from time to time. We don't know how things are going to work out, and that uncertainty creates a deep sense of discomfort.

Worry isn't a pleasant feeling or state of mind, yet we go there repeatedly. The hardest part of worrying about uncertain situations is the point where you spiral. In stressful times when we most need restorative rest, we can find ourselves lying awake in the small hours, worrying over things that we can't control. Your mind runs away with the worst-case scenario, and you feel worse and worse.

If worry doesn't make us feel good, why do we do it?

It seems to work like this. In the past, we've worried about something, but everything has turned out OK. The result is that our brain pairs the feeling of worry with a positive outcome. The brain becomes convinced that worrying helps us get the result that we want.

And sometimes it can. That dreadful feeling can motivate us into action and might help solve the problem. If we consider the fight-or-flight response, it seems likely that we evolved to experience worry in order to push us towards action when we need it.

But just like the fight-or-flight response in our modern lives, worry rarely helps at all and can actually make things harder. Severe worry is stressful. It prevents us from resting and relaxing. It hinders our ability to go about our day and take care of our lives. It takes control of our thoughts and saps our energy. [1]

[1] Sarb Johal Ph.D., D.Clin.Psy. - Crisis on Earth Posted April 23, 2021 | Reviewed by Davia Sills
https://www.psychologytoday.com/us/blog/crisis-earth/202104/why-we-worry-and-6-ways-deal-it?msockid=3b4778cfeb3b644c1ea06ab2ea5465e7

"CAREGIVERS SHOULD PRIORITIZE TASKS."

No More Worries

Giselle had always been a worrier. Growing up in the idyllic surroundings of Georgetown, Barbados, she had developed a habit of fretting over everything that crossed her mind. The smallest things—a missed deadline at work, a headache that lingered too long—could send her spiraling into anxiety. But when her parents, Adela and Tony, began to need more assistance, her worries multiplied exponentially. They were aging, and the thought of losing them or failing to care for them took a firm grip on her heart.

Adela and Tony still managed to live independently, but tasks that were once trivial—cooking, cleaning, and even grocery shopping—now became mountainous challenges that loomed over Giselle. She willingly took on the responsibility, her love for them driving her to prioritize their needs above her own. Yet, as the weeks turned into months, it became painfully clear that she was overextending herself. Her once vibrant spirit was now weighed down by an invisible burden of anxiety.

As the sun set over the Caribbean blue-green waters, Giselle found herself increasingly isolated. She rarely went out, stopped seeing her friends, and even neglected her beloved beach, a sanctuary where she once found solace and joy. The vibrant blues and greens of the sea that had once brought her peace now felt like a distant memory, overshadowed by her spiraling thoughts.

One evening, while preparing dinner, her mother, Adela, noticed the deep lines of worry etched on Giselle's face. Setting aside the chopping board, Adela gently urged her to sit down. "Giselle," she began, her voice soft yet firm, "I've noticed you've been worrying a lot lately. Is everything okay?"

Giselle sighed, the weight of her emotions spilling over. "I don't know, Mom. I'm just so worried about you and Dad. What if something happens? What if I can't take care of you anymore?"

Adela took her daughter's hands in hers, warmth radiating from her touch. "I understand your concern, sweetie. But you can't let worrying control your life. You need to take care of yourself, too. You can't pour from an empty cup."

Giselle nodded, her heart aching with the truth of her mother's words. Yet, the question remained—how could she stop? That very night, as she lay in bed, her mind raced with thoughts of what could go wrong. The more she worried, the more difficult it became to see a way out.

The following week, a turning point arrived when Tony, while tending to his garden, tripped and fell. The sight of her father on the ground sent Giselle's imagination into overdrive. What if he had broken something? What if he couldn't get back up? She raced to his side, panic coursing through her veins. But as she knelt beside him, she saw the grin on his face, a glimmer of mischief in his eyes. "Just a little tumble, sweetheart. I'll be fine," he chuckled, brushing off the dirt.

Yet, Adela, witnessing her daughter's extreme reaction, decided it was time for a heart-to-heart. "Darling," she said gently, "I understand your worry for your father, but you must remember that excessive worrying accomplishes little. It only causes unnecessary stress for yourself and those around you. Maybe it's time to seek some help."

In that moment, Giselle had an epiphany. Her worrying served no purpose; it only created a cloud of misery that enveloped her and her family. She took a deep breath, feeling the weight of realization settle on her shoulders. It was time to change.

The next day, Giselle found a local mental health support group online. Skeptical yet hopeful, she decided to attend a meeting. As she entered the cozy room filled with others who carried similar burdens, she felt an unexpected sense of relief wash over her.

Here, she was not alone. Listening to stories of struggle and resilience, she began to see a glimmer of hope.

Encouraged by the group's support, Giselle also began seeing a therapist who helped her navigate her feelings of stress and anxiety. They worked together to develop coping strategies, focusing on mindfulness and self-care techniques. Over time, she learned to harness her worries rather than let them control her.

Gradually, Giselle began to emerge from her shell. She reconnected with old friends, rediscovered her love for painting, and even returned to the beach, where the sound of waves crashing against the shore became a soothing balm for her soul. She often found herself lost in the pages of novels by R. Lee Moore, Sr., each story whisking her away to another world.

One sunny afternoon at the beach, while enjoying the gentle breeze and the salty air, Giselle's eyes fell on a handsome stranger, Roland. He was laughing with his friends, his smile lighting up the sandy stretch. Despite her initial hesitation, Giselle felt an undeniable spark of interest. They struck up a conversation about the weather—a mundane topic that blossomed into something more meaningful. Laughter and connection flowed easily between them, and soon they were spending more and more time together.

For Giselle, this budding relationship was more than just a romantic interest; it was a testament to her journey. It symbolized her ability to overcome her worries and embrace life again. Roland was understanding and patient, encouraging her to share her experiences without judgment. Through him, she learned that vulnerability could lead to strength.

As the months rolled on, Giselle transformed into a new version of herself. No longer the extreme worrier, she had found a balance between caring for her parents and nurturing her own needs. She established boundaries, ensuring she took time for herself—whether it was a day at the beach, a cozy night with a book, or a spontaneous outing with friends.

Adela and Tony, witnessing their daughter's growth, felt a renewed sense of pride. They were grateful for the care she provided but were even more grateful for the joy they saw returning to her life. Giselle had learned the invaluable lesson that worrying accomplishes little, and in sharing her journey, she hoped to inspire others to find their own paths to peace.

Today, Giselle stands at the edge of the beach, the sun setting in a blaze of orange and pink hues. She feels lighter, her heart filled with gratitude. Life is still unpredictable, but she has learned to embrace it with open arms. With Roland by her side and her parents in her heart, she continues to move forward, ready to face whatever comes next. In the end, she has discovered that it's not the worries that define us but how we choose to live in spite of them.

Why We Worry and 6 Ways to Deal With It (continued)

The good news is there are methods of dealing with these nagging feelings of dread and worry. We can't stop hurricanes, bad news, pandemics, or the clock, but it helps to acknowledge your worry and then focus on what you can control. Here's how.

1. Identify unproductive worrying.

Productive worries lead to actions that give us more control of our environment, whereas unproductive worries make us feel even more anxious and uncertain and can become a vicious cycle. Try to differentiate how much of your worrying is productive (making sure there's enough food in the house) versus unproductive (staying up all night thinking about worst case scenarios). If there's nothing you can do about it, it's not yours to worry about.

2. Express your worry.

Instead of letting the worries go round and round in your head, try keeping a worry journal. Set aside a defined period—perhaps 15 minutes—when you will give yourself full permission to worry. Write all your fears and worries down in a notebook. Once the time is up, or you've run out of worries to record, put the notebook away and let it all go.

Your worry journal can act as a parking space for unproductive worries so that they don't keep circling around your mind, looking for a space to park. Many people find that by writing it all down, they can interrupt the constant cycle of thoughts and move on, free to think about and do other things.

3. Practice mindfulness.

Try to bring moments of mindfulness into your day by sitting in active and intentional awareness. You can exercise mindfulness when sitting at the kitchen table eating your lunch: Feel the chair under your body; appreciate the texture of the food as you chew; note the sensation of going from hungry to satisfied.

Mindfulness is not easy, but it's incredibly powerful. To hone the skill, you can practice mindfulness more formally through mindfulness meditation, which trains you to better manage racing thoughts and stay grounded and present when troubling uncertainty abounds.

4. Develop habits and routines for a sense of control.

Much of the uncertainty comes from the lack of an end date to all the physical distancing, health threats, second or subsequent waves, and further lockdowns. When worry threatens to overwhelm you, it helps to recommit to your structure and routine, so you can feel a sense of control on a smaller, more individual scale. Choosing a few helpful habits, building them into your routines, and sticking to them can help tame your worry more than you realize. Habits become automatic and give us a sense of predictability and control. Plus, when we complete a task, we feel a sense of accomplishment, and that boosts our mood.

Habits and routines can help with any moment of uncertainty in life, well beyond this pandemic. Maybe you ended a relationship and feel aimless and confused about the future, or you moved across the country for a job to a town where you don't know a soul.

Not knowing how things will pan out is scary, but establishing some structure, building helpful habits into your routine, and setting small, attainable goals can help you keep going. Try setting up an activity calendar (for work and fun stuff) and sticking to it as much as possible—even when you don't feel like it and would rather crash on the couch.

5. Seek humor.

Whether it's a TV show, funny tweets, or a group chat with friends, humor is very much about the here and now. The more we're in that headspace, the less our minds travel to the future and remind us of how uncertain it is.

6. Accept what you can't control.

Acknowledging that we can't control and change everything is really important. This is easier said than done, but acceptance is a big step towards regaining peace of mind. Wanting to know and control everything fuels uncertainty, and obsessive consumption of information—grasping for certainty—can make things worse. Seeking information is vital, and keeping up with the news is important, but constantly refreshing your news and social media feeds only adds to your anxiety. [2]

Humor and Mental Health

How important is humor for a full-time caregiver?

As a full-time caregiver, the job can be tough, overwhelming and stressful. It is unlike any other job, as it requires not only a lot of physical demands but also emotional and mental ones. With all of these demands, it is crucial to find ways to relieve that built up stress and tension, and one of the best ways to do so is through humor. Humor has been found to be an effective coping mechanism when dealing with stressful situations. It is important to incorporate humor in your life as a caregiver, and this topic explores why, the benefits of humor, and examples of humor.

The benefits of using humor in caregiving

Humor can be a powerful tool for caregivers to help them cope with the daily demands of their job. It's an excellent way to cope with the daily demands and stress. Also it can help you deal with both physical and emotional pains well as relax, lift your mood, and boost your overall energy levels.

[2] Sarb Johal Ph.D., D.Clin.Psy. - Crisis on Earth Posted April 23, 2021 | Reviewed by Davia Sills
https://www.psychologytoday.com/us/blog/crisis-earth/202104/why-we-worry-and-6-ways-deal-it?msockid=3b4778cfeb3b644c1ea06ab2ea5465e7

Here are some of the benefits of humor in caregiving:

Stress reduction

Humor is a great stress buster. It helps to reduce tension, improve mood, and lower stress levels. Laughter has been found to decrease the production of stress hormones such as cortisol and adrenaline, which helps to reduce the physical symptoms of stress, such as high blood pressure, headaches, and muscle tension.

Improve Mental Health

Humor can help to improve mental health by reducing depression and anxiety. Laughter prompts the release of endorphins, which are natural mood enhancing chemicals in the body. It can also help with feelings of isolation and loneliness, which can lead to depression.

Fosters Positivity

A positive mindset is crucial in caregiving. By incorporating humor into your life, you can help to shift your mindset from negative to positive. Humor can help you see the bright side of things, even in tough situations, and help you maintain a positive attitude towards caregiving responsibilities.

Examples of humor incorporated into caregiving:

The following are examples of how humor can be incorporated into caregiving:

Jokes and humorous stories: Telling jokes or sharing humorous stories with those you care for can help brighten their day. It can also help to relieve their stress and worries, making them feel more relaxed and comfortable.

Gentle teasing: Gentle teasing can be an effective way to lighten the mood and help those you care for feel more comfortable. It can help build a deeper connection with them and show them that you genuinely care for them.

Have a daily laugh: Start your day with laughter. You can watch a funny video, tell a joke, or listen to a funny podcast. Laughter is the best medicine, and it can help you deal with the stress of caregiving.

Tell funny stories: Tell funny stories about your life or the life of the person you are caring for. You can share stories about an embarrassing moment, a funny experience, or a humorous mistake. This can help you both relax and laugh together.

Use humor in your communication

Use humor in your communication with the person you are caring for. You can use funny voices, puns, or jokes to make them laugh. This can make your communication more engaging and enjoyable for both of you.

Watch humorous videos

Watch humorous videos together with the person you are caring for. You can enjoy funny animal videos, comedy shows, or viral videos. This can bring laughter and strengthen your connection.

As a full-time caregiver, it is easy to forget about taking care of yourself. Humor is an effective way to reduce stress, boost your mood, and take care of your mental and emotional health. The benefits of incorporating humor into your caregiving routine are many, and there are many different ways to do so. By using humor, you can create a more positive overall experience for both yourself and those you care for.

Here are some jokes about caregiving that can bring a little light to the situation.

"Caregiving is like riding a roller coaster, except there's no thrill, and you're always on the ride."

"If you think caring for a toddler is tough, try caring for an adult who acts like one."

"Caregiving is like a box of chocolates: you never know what you are going to get."

"Caregiving is not for the faint hearted. It's for those who have a big heart."

"If you think caregiving is easy, try doing it without caffeine."

"The only time I get a break from caregiving is when I am asleep, and even that is not guaranteed."

Being a caregiver is an act of love and dedication that demands a lot of patience, strength, and compassion. But it doesn't always have to be a tedious job. Using funny sayings and humor in your caregiving routine can bring a lot of positive changes and lighten up the mood. Remember to have a sense of humor to make the job much more manageable.

"GENTLE TEASING CAN HELP THOSE YOU CARE FOR FEEL MORE COMFORTABLE."

Overcoming Worry in Full-Time Caregivers

Seeking Support from Family and Friends

It's essential for caregivers to have a support network to assist them navigating the challenges and stress that accompany their role. Friends, family, and other caregivers can offer both emotional and practical support.

Joining Support Groups: Joining a support group can also help caregivers feel less isolated, provide a space to share experiences, and learn coping strategies from others in similar situations.

Practicing Self-care: Caregivers need to take care of their physical and mental well-being. This includes engaging in regular physical activity, practicing mindfulness and relaxation techniques, and ensuring time for self-care and hobbies.

How To Stop Worrying, According To Experts

Can Worrying Hurt My Health?

Worrying can negatively impact health both in the short-term and long-term. As previously explained, in the short-term, worrying can cause headaches, a racing heartbeat and digestive problems. Both experts say that some people may experience panic attacks due to excessive worry.

Additionally, says Dr. Pittman, worrying can impact the immune system. She explains that psychological stress puts very real physical stress on the body, which impacts the immune system. "Worry puts the body into fight-or-flight mode and someone is not meant to stay in fight-or-flight mode for a prolonged amount of time," she says. When this does happen, Dr. Pittman says it causes inflammation in the body, which then negatively impacts the immune system. If you've ever gotten sick right after a big event or presentation at work, you've experienced the link between mental and physical stress firsthand.

Even more concerning, scientific studies show that constant worry can negatively impact heart health and even lead to premature death. Anxiety negatively impacts the cardiovascular system because it can cause the heart to beat rapidly, which interferes with normal heart function. It also raises blood pressure, which puts stress on the heart.

This is why both experts say coping with excessive worrying is important. But then comes the big question: How do you stop worrying so much?

Expert Tips for Coping With Worrying

Dr. Pittman's solution for excessive worrying comes down to three steps:

Pinpoint your worry: "First, identify what it is that you're worried about," says Dr. Pittman. For some people, it can be helpful to write this down—especially if someone is worried about several things at once. Once you identify your worry (or worries), you're ready to move on to step two.

Plan: Now that you know what you're worried about, Dr. Pittman says it's time to plan. This means asking yourself what you can do about your concerns. If you're worried about paying your bills, can you create a financial plan that includes a budget? If you're worried about everything you have to get done for the day, can you create a to do list, being specific about the times of when you will tackle each task?

Another reason why this step is important is because it helps someone identify the worries they have that are out of their control, explains Dr. Pittman. For example, you can't control what someone thinks about you. If that is your primary worry, there is no planning you can do. Once the planning is done (including if your worry is related to something you cannot plan for), it's time to move on to the last step.

Move on: When what you're worried about is out of your control—or you've done all the planning you can do connected to it—Dr. Pittman says it's time to busy yourself with something, whether it's watching TV, calling a friend or doing a hobby you enjoy. "It's important to not just tell yourself to 'stop worrying' because the brain doesn't work like that," she says. "For example, if I tell you to not think about pink elephants, all you'll be able to think about is pink elephants. You have to change the channel in your brain by thinking about something else that will replace the thought of what you're worried about."

For some people who are prone to worrying, Dr. Johnson says journaling can help. She explains that a journal can be a dedicated place to write down your worries, which some find instrumental for moving on and thinking about other things. In fact, she says that some people even block out part of their day to worry, spending roughly 20 minutes or so jotting down their worries before moving on to other tasks.

"Regular self-care is also important [for combatting worrying]," says Dr. Johnson, adding that this is because it's easier to deal with life's stressors when you take proper care of yourself. Engaging in regular exercise, eating nourishing food and spending time doing activities you enjoy are all forms of self-care.

Meditation can also be helpful for people who are prone to worrying; while worrying can cause the heart to beat faster, deep breathing and meditation is linked to slowing heart rate, taking the body out of fight-or-flight mode.

Both experts say that it can also be helpful to see a therapist if worry is consuming your life. Dr. Johnson explains that a therapist can help someone differentiate between worries they can control and worries they can't, as well as provide coping tools for when thoughts of excessive worry take over. If someone is diagnosed with generalized anxiety disorder, prescription medication (such as selective serotonin reuptake inhibitors) may also be considered.

When to Get Help

It bears repeating that worrying isn't inherently bad; some types of worrying can help keep you safe and prepared. But if worry is getting in the way of your happiness or ability to function, both experts say it's important to seek help. If you don't, excessive worrying could be detrimental to your health.

When worries are kept at bay, you're able to live the life you were meant to live; one full of joy. Worrying is synonymous with anxiety. Do you know what the opposite is? Peace. [3]

[3] https://www.forbes.com/health/mind/how-to-stop-worrying/
Written By Emily Laurence, Certified Health Coach
Sabrina Romanoff, Psy.D., Medically Reviewed

Results Over Time

Improvement in Caregiver's Physical and Mental Health

Trying to manage worry and stress can lead to improved physical and mental health for caregivers. This can include better sleep, improved immune function, and better emotional regulation.

Improved Quality of Care for the Care Receiver

Caregivers who prioritize their well-being are better equipped to provide quality care and emotional support to their loved one.

How to Handle Worry as a Full-Time Caregiver

Recognize and Acknowledge the Worry

The first step in handling worry is recognizing and acknowledging it, rather than trying to ignore it or push it aside.

Find Ways to Cope with Stress

Finding ways to cope with stress is essential in managing worry. This includes practicing relaxation techniques, engaging in regular physical activity, and finding ways to have fun and enjoy life outside of the caregiver role.

Focus on Positive Aspects of Caregiving

Caregiving can be a rewarding and fulfilling experience.

Focusing on the positive aspects of the role can help caregivers combat negative emotions and foster a sense of gratitude and purpose.

Finally, as a full-time caregiver, worry can have profound effects on a caregiver's physical, emotional, and social well-being. Recognizing the causes of worry in full-time caregivers and finding ways to overcome it can lead to improved health outcomes for both the caregiver and care receiver. Caregivers should prioritize self-care, seek out social support, and focus on the positive aspects of the caregiver role.

Frequently Asked Questions:

How can I tell if I am an over worrier?

If you find that you worry excessively about things to the point where it affects your daily life, it may be a sign of being an over-worrier.

How can I seek help for my excessive worrying?

One can seek help through professional therapy, online support groups, or talking to friends and family members.

Is isolation and avoidance common symptoms of excessive worrying?

Yes, for many people, worrying can lead to avoiding or isolating oneself, often due to the fear of the worst case scenario.

What methods can I use to overcome my worrying habits?

One can overcome worrying habits by challenging negative thoughts, practicing mindfulness meditation, and seeking professional help.

Chapter 4 — Detachment

Emotionally Detaching From Those Around Us

Taking care of others is a noble and often selfless task that requires a great deal of physical, emotional, and mental energy. However, in the midst of all the love and dedication, there may come a time when caregiving causes emotional burnout. Sometimes, caregivers become so overwhelmed by their emotions that they are unable to properly care for others and themselves.One way to deal with this issue is by learning how to detach emotionally when necessary. On this topic, we'll explore the question of whether caregivers should learn to detach emotionally from those we care for and others around us. We'll also discuss how to detach and the best methods for learning this valuable skill.

What is emotional detachment?

Emotional detachment is a coping mechanism that helps individuals disengage from overly emotional situations or people. It can help us avoid becoming overwhelmed or feeling burnt out, and allow us to maintain a level headed perspective.

Detachment does not mean we completely disconnect or stop caring for others. It is just a simple way to maintain a healthy emotional distance for self-preservation.

Reasons to detach emotionally

Emotional detachment is beneficial in several situations, such as when:

- One needs to cope with overwhelming emotions
- The caregiver needs to take a break from caring for others
- The caregiver has a limited capacity for handling emotional stress
- There is potential danger of developing caregiver burnout
- There are boundary issues between the caregiver and the person being cared for
- Dealing with difficult patients who may be unpleasant or even abusive

Should caregivers detach emotionally?

It is okay for caregivers to detach emotionally from those we care for, as it can be empowering to maintain our boundaries and take care of ourselves. Caregivers have to focus on self-care, too, and that means taking care of their mental and emotional well-being.

However, it is important to note that the level of detachment should always be appropriate for the situation, keeping in mind that some levels of attachment are necessary for effective caregiving.

"DETACHMENT DOES NOT MEAN WE COMPLETELY DISCONNECT."

MOM, Stop Calling Me!

Dolores sat at her kitchen table, the sun streaming through the window, casting warm rays over the clutter of bills and half finished projects. She stared blankly at her phone, the screen illuminating the latest message from her mother, Beatrice. It was another request, another demand that felt more like a weight pressing down on her chest.

"Are you going to the store?" the message read, sent only five minutes after the last one.

Dolores sighed, rubbing her temples. It had become a cycle of endless neediness from Beatrice. Just yesterday, the calls had started early.

"Dolores, can you come in here?" Beatrice's voice echoed from her bedroom, laced with urgency.

"Mom, what do you need?" Dolores shouted back, already knowing it would be some trivial matter.

"I was just wondering if you were going to the store," Beatrice replied, her tone almost whiny.

Dolores felt her irritation simmering at the surface. "I just went last night, Mom. I brought you groceries."

"Oh, right. Well, can you get me something good to eat?" Beatrice continued, her voice rising in pitch.

"Mom, I just brought you food. It's in the fridge!" Dolores felt her patience beginning to fray. This was the fifth time in thirty minutes her mother had called her for something mundane.

"Okay, okay, I'll check," Beatrice said, but Dolores could hear the disappointment in her tone.

As she walked to the fridge, a wave of despair washed over her. How had it come to this? Beatrice was no longer the strong, independent woman she once knew. Now, she was a shadow of herself—dependent, anxious, and demanding. Dolores felt like she was drowning under the weight of her mother's needs.

That evening, Dolores sat down with a glass of wine, the cool liquid a temporary reprieve from her thoughts. She knew she needed to change her approach, but how? As she pondered, her phone buzzed again.

"Are you going to church tomorrow?" Beatrice asked, her message popping up like a new task to complete.

Dolores took a deep breath, her chest tight with anxiety. "Mom, it's Thursday. Church isn't until Sunday."

"Oh, right. I just don't feel well. I might need you to come by."

The request felt like a punch to the gut. Dolores had been planning to take the weekend for herself, maybe catch up on reading, or even just relax without the constant demands. Instead, it seemed she would be spending it in her mother's room, catering to her whims like a servant.

"Mom, I can't keep coming over every time you feel a little off," Dolores said, her voice steady but firm.

"What do you mean?" Beatrice sounded genuinely confused.

"I mean that I need some time for myself too. I can't just drop everything whenever you call," Dolores replied, her heart racing.

"Dolores, you know I rely on you," Beatrice said, her voice tinged with guilt.

"I know, Mom. But you need to find ways to manage on your own, too. I can't be your only support," Dolores said, feeling a flicker of resolve.

As days turned into weeks, Dolores began to practice emotional detachment. She started with small steps, like letting the phone ring instead of rushing to answer every time. She found herself saying, "No," more often, allowing guilt to wash over her but refusing to let it dictate her actions.

One evening, Beatrice called again. "Dolores, can you bring me some soup? I'm not feeling well."

Dolores paused, feeling the familiar pull of obligation. But then she took a breath, centered herself, and replied, "Mom, I can't. I have plans tonight."

"What plans?" Beatrice asked, her voice rising slightly.

"I'm going to meet some friends. It's important for me to take time for myself," Dolores said, her heart pounding as she spoke the words.

"Friends? You should be here taking care of me," Beatrice snapped, the frustration evident in her tone.

Dolores felt the old guilt creeping in, but she pushed it down. "I will help you, Mom, but I can't be your only source of support. You have neighbors, and there are services available."

Beatrice fell silent, the weight of the conversation hanging in the air. "I just don't want to be alone," she finally said, her voice softer.

Dolores's heart ached at the vulnerability in her mother's words. "I understand, and I'm here for you. But you also need to find ways to be okay on your own. I believe you can do it."

Weeks passed, and while Beatrice still called, the frequency of her requests diminished. Dolores found herself more centered, more at peace as she embraced her own life. She discovered the joy of saying no without guilt, of prioritizing her own needs without apology.

One Saturday, Dolores had planned a day out, a small adventure she had been looking forward to for weeks. As she prepared to leave, Beatrice called.

"Dolores, are you busy today?"

Dolores took a moment, feeling the old instinct to rush to her mother's side, but she gently pushed it aside. "I am, actually. I'm going out for the day."

"Oh," Beatrice replied, her voice lacking its usual edge. "Okay."

Dolores felt a mix of triumph and tenderness. "I'll check in later, okay? I love you."

"I love you too," Beatrice said, and this time, there was a note of acceptance in her voice.

As Dolores stepped outside, she felt the warmth of the sun on her face, a symbol of her newfound freedom. She had learned to detach, not out of a lack of love but out of a necessity to care for herself. And in doing so, she had given her mother the space to grow, too. It was a delicate balance, but one worth striving for.

How to detach emotionally

Here are some tips on how caregivers can learn to detach emotionally when necessary:

Set boundaries: Establish clear boundaries to prevent being overwhelmed or stretched too thin. Boundaries can serve as a safeguard against stress, negativity, and burnout.

Develop a support system: Seek out those who understand the challenges of caregiving and can offer support and guidance.

Take time for oneself: It's important to take breaks and invest in activities that promote relaxation and mindfulness.

Practice mindfulness: Mindfulness is one of the best self-care practices that can help individuals detach from volatile emotions and reactions.

Practice positive self-talk: Positive self-talk helps to shift attention away from negative thoughts and emotions, and fosters a stronger emotional and mental resilience.

Benefits of emotional detachment

Emotional detachment has several benefits, including:

- It helps to reduce stress and burnout

- It fosters emotional and mental strength

- It helps create healthy boundaries between caregivers and patients- It helps to reduce stress and burnout

- It increases the caregiver's control over their emotions and enhances their overall well-being.

Risks of emotional detachment

Like any coping mechanism, emotional detachment can have consequences if don't strike a healthy balance. If you detach too much, there's a risk of becoming too emotionally disconnected from those around you. This kind of detachment can lead to apathy and disconnection, which can damage relationships and interpersonal connections.

Balancing emotional detachment and attachment

Emotional detachment is not an all-or-nothing approach for caregivers. It's important to find the right balance between emotional attachment and detachment. It's healthy for caregivers to acknowledge their emotions, but they should also learn when and how to release these emotions in a healthy way.

Furthermore, caregiving is essential work, but it becomes a nearly impossible task when a caregiver's emotions become overwhelming. Learning how to emotionally detach can benefit a caregiver in several ways, allowing them to maintain healthy boundaries and avoid burnout.

However, it's important to remember that emotional detachment is not the only solution. Striking the right balance between attachment and detachment is crucial to ensure healthy relationships with those we care for.

Frequently Asked Questions:

Is it normal to have difficulty detaching emotionally from my relatives or patients as a caregiver?

Yes, it's normal. Caregivers often experience a range of emotions when caring for others, including empathy, stress, and overwhelm. However, developing emotional detachment can help maintain relationships while taking care of yourself.

How can I tell if I'm emotionally detached from those I care for?

If you find yourself feeling nothing for those you care for or feel disconnected from them, you may be experiencing emotional detachment. However, it's important to distinguish emotional detachment from burnout, which can cause similar symptoms.

Can emotional detachment be harmful for caregivers or the cared for?

If emotional detachment is taken too far, it can become harmful, and ultimately damaging to relationships. Emotional detachment should be balanced and appropriate for the situation and should not be used as an excuse for neglect or unkindness.

Are there any other ways to cope with caregiver burnout?

Yes, other ways to cope with caregiver burnout include self-care, practicing stress reduction techniques like meditation, exercise, and setting achievable goals. Seeking out support groups or a therapist can also help caregivers dealing with burnout.

"CAREGIVERS DO MATTER."

CAREGIVERS BILL OF RIGHTS

The Components of the Caregiver's Bill of Rights

The Caregiver's Bill of Rights is made up of five components that empower caregivers to take care of themselves while providing care to their loved ones.

These rights include:

• *Right to Self-Care*

Caregivers have a right to take care of their physical and emotional health needs. Taking care of yourself is essential to ensure that you remain healthy and are capable of providing care in the long-term.

• *Right to Seek Assistance*

Taking care of someone with a health issue or disability can be challenging, and caregivers need to have access to resources and support when they need it. This right provides caregivers with the opportunity to seek assistance from family members, medical professionals, and community resources.

• *Right to Balance*

Caregiving can be a full-time job, and it's essential to achieve a balance between your responsibilities as a caregiver and your personal life. This right encourages caregivers to seek out activities that bring them joy and fulfillment outside of caregiving.

• *Right to Respect*

Caregivers have a right to respect from their loved ones and medical professionals. Their opinions and views on the care of their loved ones should be considered when creating care plans.

• *Right to Information*

Caregivers need to have access to information about their loved ones' medical condition and care plan. This right encourages healthcare professionals to provide caregivers with information that will help them provide the best care possible.

How the Caregiver's Bill of Rights Can Improve Caregiving

Implementing the Caregiver's Bill of Rights can improve caregiving in several ways, including:

Improving Overall Health and Well being

Caregivers who practice self-care and seek assistance when needed are more likely to remain healthy and avoid burnout.

Improved Caregiver-Recipient Relationship

Caregivers who have access to resources and support are better equipped to provide quality care to their loved ones, improving the caregiver-recipient relationship.

Reduced Caregiver Burnout and Stress

Taking care of your physical and emotional health needs can reduce stress and burnout, making caregiving more manageable in the long-term.

The Caregiver's Bill of Rights provides a framework that supports family caregivers and promotes their rights to take care of themselves while caring for their loved ones. These rights can improve care recipients' health outcomes, improve caregiver recipient relationships, and reduce caregiver stress and burnout.

If you are a caregiver, make sure you familiarize yourself with these rights, and don't be afraid to advocate for your needs. By taking care of yourself, you can provide better care for your loved ones.

Maximizing the Guide into your Journey

To maximize this guide, we recommend:

- Dedicate regular time to reflect on the information and your experiences.

- Use the guide as a resource for support.

- Connect with support groups or online communities for encouragement.

- Celebrate small victories and acknowledge your growth.

Remember, overcoming anxiety, stress, and worry is a gradual process. Be patient with yourself, practice self-compassion, and utilize the resources to enhance your mental health and overall well-being.

My hope is that this book has illuminated the emotional struggles of full-time caregivers. In this guide, I've explored the causes and effects of anxiety, stress, and worry with suggestions for overcoming them.

The importance of self-care is emphasized, and I recognize the vital role caregivers play in our society. The insights shared here aim to empower caregivers to address their emotional challenges and prioritize mental health.

This guide serves as a resource for adopting a mindful approach to self-care and fostering supportive communities, helping caregivers improve their well-being and care for their loved ones.

We aspire for this guide to contribute to a healthier society for caregivers. *Caregivers DO Matter!*

www.**Moore**BooksR.us

OVERCOMING...

A Caregiver's Guide

Explore the emotional struggles and challenges faced by full-time caregivers, delving into the causes, effects, and strategies for overcoming feelings of frustration, anger, stress, guilt and exhaustion. These guides also underscore the vital importance of self-care.

It is essential to acknowledge the immense role that caregivers play in our society, highlighting their personal sacrifices and the profound impact they have on the lives of those they care for. The knowledge shared will serve as a guide for caregivers to embrace a mindful approach to self-care and cultivate supportive communities, fostering improved well-being and enhanced care for their loved ones.

The ultimate goal of this book is to contribute to a healthier, more compassionate society that values the crucial work of caregivers.

Remember, *Caregivers DO Matter.*

OVERCOMING

- Frustration, Anger & Exhaustion
- Lonliness, Abandonment,
  & Depression
- Anxiety, Worry, & Stress
- Guilt. Grief, & Regret

www.MooreBooksR.us

Think Feel Speak Write — Do 2.o

A Path Toward Realizing Your Purpose

Many of us are frustrated, confused, and lack enthusiasm; just going through the motions in life. We have settled for the world's definition of who we are instead of agreeing with God who has created us on purpose.

In this book are insights and stories that offer a fresh outlook on how these principles can impact your journey. You too may find that as you Think, Feel, Speak, Write, and DO purposefully, you can live a fulfilling life as God created you to live, with purpose.

Get started today!

www.onecreativemindllc.com/think2 or thinkfeelspeakwritedo2.com

---

"Why Won't They Just Die!"

"Emotional turmoil of Caregivers often goes unnoticed."

When a caregiver experiences the thought, "why won't they just die!" they are not actually expressing a wish for the death of their loved one. It's used in a time when the caregiver feels that they've reached their limit; in a moment of overwhelm, frustration and desperation, where they feel like they're running out of options.

www.whywonttheyjustdie.com

Contact R. Lee Moore, Sr.

For Book Signings &
Speaking Engagements:

RLeeMooreSr@gmail.com
(844) 246-2200
www.RonaldLeeMooreSr.com

R. Lee Moore, Sr.
295 E. Swedesford Road, #288
Wayne, PA 19087

www.**Moore**BooksR.us

www.ingramcontent.com/pod-product-compliance
Lightning Source LLC
Chambersburg PA
CBHW051229120626
46547CB00013B/1571